5 Ingredient Slow

Cooking

for Two

50 Healthy

Two-Serving

5 Ingredient Slow

Cooker Recipes

Louise Davidson

ISBN: 978-1718758735

Printed in the United States

Contents

Introduction

A slow cooker is a modern kitchen appliance designed to provide the ultimate cooking convenience. Three words that perfectly describe a slow cooker are durable, versatile, and portable. It lets you prepare all types of meals without demanding much of your time. Slow cooking takes many hours to prepare aromatic, healthy cuisine, but only a few minutes of your time. All you need to do is to add the specified recipe ingredients, close its lid, set the cooking time, and that's it.

A slow cooker is a healthy way of preparing food, as it preserves maximum nutrients including minerals, proteins, vitamins, and anti-oxidants. Slow cooked meals are truly nutritious and delicious for our body. Rich with essential nutrients, these meals are sure to keep you going.

Five-ingredient Cooking
Our hectic work life makes it hard for homemakers and working couples alike to find time to complete day-to-day errands. We are always in a rush to get things done, and extra time seems like a true luxury. Everyone's on the lookout for smart hacks that give them more time to spend with each other.

This book provides an exclusive collection of healthy and delicious slow cooker recipes to prepare from just five ingredients for two people. When you need only five ingredients to make delicious recipes, it's quick and easy to prepare your meal. Please note, there are a few ingredients (such as pepper, salt, cooking oils, butter, broths, stocks, and water) that form the basis for most recipes. We have not counted them as part of the five.

1

Essential Slow Cooking Tips

- When the cooking time is over, do not forget to turn off your slow cooker. If it is left on then it might overcook (or even burn) the food.
- Always keep the base of a slow cooker on a clean, dry surface, to avoid any risk of electric shock. A thick wooden cutting board will protect your counter from the heat.
- While stirring or mixing the ingredients, avoid using metal utensils. You can use any heat-proof plastic, silicone, or wooden utensils to prevent scratching of the base.
- After you are done cooking, use a soft, damp cloth and warm, soapy water to clean the base. Avoid using abrasive scrubbing pads.
- To remove residue and stains, you can either use a dampened cloth, a sponge, or a rubber spatula. A soak with warm water, vinegar, and baking soda will help.
- The lid should be washed with soapy water.

The book covers 50 healthy and easy slow cooker recipes for two, right from breakfast to desserts. The book includes dedicated chapters on breakfast foods, chicken, turkey, beef, lamb, pork, seafood, vegetarian/vegan, and dessert recipes to fulfill all your many cooking needs.

Get ready to explore the exciting world of slow cooking. Let's get started!

Breakfast Recipes

Strawberry French Toast

Servings: 2 - Prep. time: 10 minutes - Cooking time: 2 ½ h or 6 h

Ingredients:
1 teaspoon butter, melted
2 medium-sized eggs
½ cup 2% milk
1 teaspoon vanilla extract
⅛ teaspoon sea salt
4 slices whole grain bread, crusts removed, cut in 1-inch cubes
2 cups strawberries
2 ounces low-fat cream cheese, cut in small chunks

Preparation:
1. Grease the inside cooking surface of the slow cooker using the butter.
2. In a large bowl, thoroughly whisk the eggs, milk, vanilla, and salt.
3. Add the bread cubes and toss to mix; set aside for 3–4 minutes so the bread can soak up the egg.
4. Arrange half of the bread mixture in the cooker. Top with the strawberries and cream cheese.
5. Top with the remaining bread mixture.
6. Close the lid, and cook on LOW for 6 hours, or 2 ½ hours on HIGH.
7. Divide among serving bowls or plates, and enjoy!

Nutrition facts per serving
Calories 389, Carbs 40.3 g, Fat 10.2 g, Protein 17 g, Sodium 604 mg

Salmon Casserole Breakfast

Servings: 2 - Prep. time: 8–10 minutes - Cooking time: 8 hours

Ingredients:
2 eggs
1 cup 2% milk
1 teaspoon dried dill
Freshly ground black pepper to taste
⅛ teaspoon sea salt
1 teaspoon butter
2 medium-sized russet potatoes, peeled and thinly sliced
4 ounces smoked salmon

Preparation:
1. In a mixing bowl, whisk the eggs, milk, dill, pepper, and salt.
2. Set your slow cooker on a dry kitchen platform, and grease the inside cooking surface using the butter.
3. Arrange a third of the potatoes in a layer on the bottom of the cooker
4. Top with a third of the salmon, and pour a third of the egg mixture over it.
5. Repeat the layers in the same manner.
6. Close the lid, and set slow cooking time to 8 hours on LOW.
7. Divide among serving bowls or plates, and enjoy!

Nutrition facts per serving
Calories 354, Carbs 38.8 g, Fat 5 g, Protein 24.2 g, Sodium 1291 mg

Yogurt Mango Breakfast Bowl

*Servings: 2 (store leftovers in the fridge for later) –
Prep. time: 8–10 minutes - Cooking time: 10 hours*

Ingredients:

4 cups 2% milk
¼ cup plain yogurt with live cultures
2 mangos, diced
1 tablespoon honey
¼ teaspoon cardamom, ground

Preparation:

1. Place the milk in the slow cooker, close the lid, and cook for 2 hours on LOW.
2. Turn off the cooker and stir the yogurt in with the milk.
3. Close the lid and wrap the outside of the cooker housing with a large towel, in order to insulate it.
4. Allow it to rest overnight, or for 8 hours.
5. To serve, divide the mix into serving bowls.
6. Mix in the mango chunks, honey, and cardamom.
7. Refrigerate any leftovers.

Nutrition facts per serving

Calories 207, Carbs 31 g, Fat 3.2 g, Protein 9.4 g, Sodium 128 mg

Fruity Quinoa Morning

Servings: 2 - Prep. time: 5–8 minutes - Cooking time: 8 hours

Ingredients:
2 cups fresh fruit of your choice (berries, peaches, apples, etc.)
¾ cup quinoa
⅛ teaspoon sea salt
1 teaspoon vanilla extract
3 cups water
2 tablespoons toasted pecans

Preparation:
1. In your slow cooker, combine the fruit, quinoa and salt.
2. Add the vanilla extract and water.
3. Stir the ingredients gently to combine well using a wooden spatula.
4. Close the lid, and set the time to 8 hours on LOW.
5. Divide among serving bowls and top with the toasted pecans.
6. Serve warm!

Nutrition facts per serving
Calories 321, Carbs 52 g, Fat 1.3 g, Protein 11.2 g, Sodium122 mg

Milky Pear Oatmeal

Servings: 2 - Prep. time: 5–8 minutes - Cooking time: 6–8 hours

Ingredients:
1 pear, seeded and sliced
½ teaspoon maple extract
½ teaspoon vanilla extract
2 cups milk
½ cup steel cut oats
1 cup water
Optional: chopped walnuts, for garnish

Preparation:
1. Combine all the ingredients in your slow cooker. Stir gently to combine.
2. Cover, and cook for 6–8 hours on LOW.
3. Top with some chopped walnuts (optional), and serve.

Nutrition facts per serving
Calories 257, Carbs 14 g, Fat 24 g, Protein 4.5 g, Sodium 132 mg

Chicken & Poultry Recipes

Tomato Turkey Chili

Servings: 2 - Prep. time: 5–8 minutes - Cooking time: 8 hours

Ingredients:
½ pound ground turkey
½ cup diced fire-roasted tomatoes
1 green jalapeños chili, chopped
1 small white onion, chopped
3 tablespoons tomato purée
1 cup beef broth
Salt and pepper to taste
Optional: sour cream and chopped chives, for serving

Preparation:
1. Heat a non-stick skillet over medium.
2. Add the ground turkey, cook and stir continuously for 4-5 minutes to brown evenly.
3. Drain off any grease and add the meat to a slow cooker.
4. Add the remaining ingredients, and season with salt and pepper.
5. Cover, and cook on LOW for 8 hours.
6. Plate, and serve with sour cream and chives, if desired.

Nutrition facts per serving
Calories 298, Carbs 12.3 g, Fat 14 g, Protein 33 g, Sodium 607 mg

Poultry Veggie Delight

Servings: 2 (refrigerate leftovers) - Prep. time: 5–8 minutes – Cooking time: 7–8 hours

Ingredients:
1 small head cauliflower, cut into florets
12 ounces ground turkey
2 cups peas, frozen and thawed
2 cups carrots, peeled and chopped
2 tablespoons tomato paste
⅓ cup water
Black pepper and salt to taste
Cooking spray

Preparation:
1. In the slow cooker, combine the turkey, peas, carrots, tomato paste and water.
2. Season with black pepper and salt, and stir the ingredients gently to combine well using a wooden spatula.
3. Cover, and cook on LOW for 8 hours.
4. In the meantime, in a saucepan over high heat, steam the cauliflower until it is very tender.
5. Drain the water, and mash the cauliflower using a spoon or potato masher.
6. Thirty minutes before you are ready to eat, open the slow cooker and add the cauliflower. Cover, and cook until heated through.
7. Serve.

Nutrition facts per serving
Calories 307, Carbs 4 g, Fat 19.4 g, Protein 21.6 g, Sodium 543 mg

Cranberry Sweet Chicken

*Servings: 2 (refrigerate leftovers) - Prep. time: 5 –8 minutes –
Cooking time: 7 to 7 ½ hours*

Ingredients:
1 cup cranberries
4 boneless, skinless chicken thighs
1 cup cranberries
¼ cup tomato ketchup
1 tablespoon sugar
2 teaspoons Dijon mustard
Cooking spray

Preparation:
1. Spray the inside of the slow cooker with cooking spray.
2. Add the cranberries and place the chicken on top.
3. In a mixing bowl, mix the remaining ingredients together, and pour over the chicken.
4. Cover, and cook on LOW for 7 to 7 ½ hours.
5. Serve.

Nutrition facts per serving
Calories 168, Carbs 8.4 g, Fat 28 g, Protein 25.7 g, Sodium 386 mg

Chicken Tomatino

Servings: 2 - Prep. time: 5–8 minutes - Cooking time: 8 hours

Ingredients:
1 teaspoon olive oil, extra virgin
4 garlic cloves, minced
Zest of 1 lemon
1 pint grape tomatoes 4 garlic cloves, minced
1 pound bone-in, skinless chicken thighs
1 teaspoon thyme
⅛ teaspoon sea salt
Black pepper as needed

Preparation:
1. Grease the inside surface of the slow cooker using the olive oil.
2. Arrange the garlic, zest, and tomatoes in the bottom.
3. Place the chicken on the tomato mixture, and season with the thyme, salt, and pepper.
4. Cover, and cook on LOW for 8 hours.
5. Serve hot.

Nutrition facts per serving
Calories 378, Carbs 10.3 g, Fat 1 g, Protein 27.8 g, Sodium 457 mg

Barbecue Cheddar Chicken

Servings: 2 - Prep. time: 5–8 minutes - Cooking time: 3 hours

Ingredients:
2 chicken breasts
1 cup spicy barbecue sauce
Salt and pepper to taste
2 ounce sharp cheddar cheese, shredded

Preparation:
1. Place the chicken in the slow cooker.
2. Top with the barbecue sauce and season to taste with salt and pepper. Stir the ingredients gently to combine, using a wooden spatula.
3. Cover, and cook on HIGH for 3 hours.
4. After 2 hours and 45 minutes, open the lid and top with the cheese.
5. Close the lid; cook on "HIGH" for 15 minutes, until the cheese is melted.
6. Serve, and enjoy!

Nutrition facts per serving
Calories 291, Carbs 5.2 g, Fat 17 g, Protein 29 g, Sodium 426 mg

Sherry Mushroom Chicken

Servings: 2 - Prep. time: 10 minutes - Cooking time: 7–8 hours

Ingredients:
1 teaspoon unsalted butter
2 cups cremini mushrooms, thinly sliced
2 garlic cloves, minced
1 shallot, minced
3 tablespoons dry sherry
2 skinless, bone-in chicken thighs, about 6 ounces each
⅛ teaspoon sea salt
Black pepper to taste
Rice or mashed potato, for serving

Preparation:
1. Grease the inside cooking surface of the slow cooker with the butter.
2. Add the mushrooms, garlic, and shallot, and toss gently.
3. Pour in the sherry.
4. Season the chicken with salt and pepper, and place them on top of the mushroom mixture. Stir briefly.
5. Cover, and cook on LOW for 7–8 hours.
6. Serve hot with your choice of rice or potato.

Nutrition facts per serving
Calories 207, Carbs 5.3 g, Fat 2 g, Protein 24.2 g, Sodium 236 mg

Chicken Sausage Feast

Servings: 2 - Prep. time: 5–8 minutes - Cooking time: 8 hours

Ingredients:
1 teaspoon olive oil
2 skinless, bone-in chicken thighs, about 8 ounces each
½ fennel bulb, cored and thinly sliced
½ red onion, halved and thinly sliced
⅛ teaspoon sea salt
1 hot Italian sausage link, casing removed

Preparation:
1. Grease the inside cooking surface of the slow cooker with the olive oil.
2. Add the chicken, fennel, onion, and salt. Stir the ingredients gently to combine.
3. Crumble the sausage and spread it around the chicken.
4. Cover, and cook on LOW for 8 hours.
5. Serve hot.

Nutrition facts per serving
Calories 339, Carbs 7.2 g, Fat 1 g, Protein 24 g, Sodium 294 mg

Chicken Coconut Curry

Servings: 2 - Prep. time: 10 minutes - Cooking time: 3 ½ hours

Ingredients:
1 medium red onion, peeled and sliced
1 teaspoon garlic, minced
4-5 large chicken thighs, skinless
Salt and pepper to taste
½ cup full-fat coconut milk
1 teaspoon curry powder
Cooking spray
Bread or steamed rice, for serving

Preparation:
1. Grease the inside cooking surface of your slow cooker using a cooking oil spray.
2. Arrange the onion and garlic inside.
3. Top with the chicken thighs, and season with salt and pepper.
4. In a mixing bowl, combine the coconut milk and curry powder; pour this mixture over the chicken.
5. Cook on HIGH for 3 to 3 ½ hours.
6. When the time is up, open the lid and take out only the chicken.
7. Shred the chicken meat from the bones, and cut it into bite-sized pieces. Discard the bones.
8. Return the chicken to the cooker, and combine it with the cooking liquid.
9. Serve with bread or a cup of steamed rice.

Nutrition facts per serving
Calories 351, Carbs 6.2 g, Fat 28.4 g, Protein 26 g, Sodium 384 mg

Chicken with Mozzarella & Peppers

Servings: 2 - Prep. time: 5–8 minutes - Cooking time: 7–8 hours

Ingredients:
1 teaspoon olive oil
2 boneless skinless chicken breasts
Salt and pepper to taste
2 roasted red bell peppers, thinly sliced
2 ounces mozzarella cheese, sliced
¼ cup basil, roughly chopped

Preparation:
1. Grease the inside of the slow cooker surface with the olive oil.
2. Season the chicken with salt and pepper, and arrange it in the cooker.
3. Top with the peppers and sliced cheese, and sprinkle the basil on the top.
4. Cover, and cook on LOW for 7–8 hours.
5. Serve hot.

Nutrition facts per serving
Calories 384, Carbs 8 g, Fat 6 g, Protein 48.7 g, Sodium 416 mg

Pearl Mushroom Chicken

Servings: 2 - Prep. time: 10 minutes - Cooking time: 8 hours

Ingredients:
1 teaspoon olive oil
12 ounces skinless chicken breasts, bone in
1 cup blanched pearl onions
6 button mushrooms, quartered
1 teaspoon garlic, minced
⅛ teaspoon sea salt
Black pepper to taste
1 cup dry white wine
Optional: egg noodles or brown rice, for serving.

Preparation:
1. Grease the inside cooking surface of the slow cooker with the olive oil.
2. Arrange the chicken in the cooker, and toss the onions, mushrooms, and garlic on top of the chicken.
3. Season with salt and pepper. Pour in the wine.
4. Cover, and cook on LOW for 8 hours.
5. Serve hot with egg noodles or brown rice.

Nutrition facts per serving
Calories 414, Carbs 11 g, Fat 1.2 g, Protein 51.3 g, Sodium 244 mg

Beef Recipes

Rosemary Veggie Roast

Servings: 2 - Prep. time: 5–8 minutes - Cooking time: 8 hours

Ingredients:
1 pound chuck roast, trimmed of fat
⅛ teaspoon sea salt
Black pepper to taste
1 onion, cut in wedges
2 carrots, cut in 2-inch pieces
2 red potatoes, quartered
1 teaspoon fresh rosemary, minced
1 cup low-sodium beef broth

Preparation:
1. Season the roast with the salt and pepper.
2. Place the roast in the slow cooker, and arrange the vegetables around it.
3. Sprinkle the rosemary over everything, and pour the stock in around the roast.
4. Cook on LOW for 8 hours.
5. Serve hot.

Nutrition facts per serving
Calories 694, Carbs 46.2 g, Fat 7.3 g, Protein 76.4 g, Sodium 526 mg

Barbecue Mustard Beef

Servings: 2 - Prep. time: 5–8 minutes - Cooking time: 8 hours

Ingredients:
2 beef short ribs, bone in and cut into single rib pieces
Salt and pepper to taste
¼ cup beef stock
½ cup barbecue sauce
1 tablespoon mustard
1 tablespoon green onions, chopped

Preparation:
1. Season the ribs with salt and pepper, and arrange them in the slow cooker.
2. In a small mixing bowl, combine the beef stock, barbecue sauce, and mustard. Pour the mixture over the beef.
3. Cook on LOW for 8 hours.
4. Transfer the meat to serving plates, and top with green onion.

Nutrition facts per serving
Calories 286, Carbs 21.3 g, Fat 5 g, Protein 6.7 g, Sodium 612 mg

Barley Carrot Beef Soup

Servings: 2 - Prep. time: 5–8 minutes - Cooking time: 8 hours

Ingredients:
1 cup diced onion
1 cup diced carrot
8 ounces beef stew meat, trimmed of fat and cut in small pieces
¼ cup pearl barley
1 teaspoon thyme
2 cups low-sodium beef stock
⅛ teaspoon sea salt

Preparation:
1. Combine all the ingredients in your slow cooker.
2. Cook on LOW for 8 hours.
3. Serve, and enjoy!

Nutrition facts per serving
Calories 412, Carbs 25 g, Fat 14.8 g, Protein 48.2 g, Sodium 311 mg

Spiced Beef Lettuce Wraps

Servings: 2 - Prep. time: 5–8 minutes - Cooking time: 4 or 8 hours

Ingredients:
Cooking spray
½ pound beef roast, trimmed from apparent fat
1 red bell pepper, trimmed and sliced thinly
½ cup red onion, sliced
½ teaspoon sea salt
2 tablespoons garam masala
4-6 large lettuce leaves

Preparation:
1. Grease the inside cooking surface of your slow cooker with cooking spray.
2. Add all the ingredients EXCEPT the lettuce, and mix gently.
3. Cook on HIGH for 3 hours, or on LOW for 6 hours.
4. When the time is almost up, remove the beef and shred it using forks.
5. Place the meat back in the cooker until the time is finished.
6. Serve warm, wrapped in the lettuce leaves.

Nutrition facts per serving
Calories 402, Carbs 13 g, Fat 23 g, Protein 34 g, Sodium 687 mg

Cheesy Eggplant Beef

Servings: 2 - Prep. time: 5–8 minutes - Cooking time: 4 h 30 min

Ingredients:
1 medium-sized eggplant, stem removed and cut in large chunks
1 pound ground beef
1 ½ tablespoons Italian spice mix
Salt and pepper to taste
1 ½ tomatoes, chopped
1 cup mozzarella cheese, shredded
Cooking spray

Preparation:
1. Grease the inside cooking surface of the slow cooker with cooking spray.
2. Arrange the eggplant inside the cooker.
3. In a bowl, mix the ground beef and the Italian spice blend, and season with salt and pepper.
4. Crumble this mixture over the eggplant. Mix in the tomato, and combine well.
5. Cook on LOW for 4 hours.
6. Just before the time is up, open the lid and add the cheese.
7. Cover, and cook until the cheese is melted.
8. Divide among serving bowls or plates, and enjoy!

Nutrition facts per serving
Calories 412, Carbs 6.3 g, Fat 22.4 g, Protein 38 g, Sodium 328 mg

Apple Cider Pot Roast

Servings: 2 - Prep. time: 5–8 minutes - Cooking time: 4 hours

Ingredients:

8 ounces beef pot roast, trimmed and cut in small pieces
Salt and pepper to taste
½ teaspoon onion powder
¼ cup apple cider vinegar
½ teaspoon minced garlic
½ cup tomato ketchup
Cooking spray

Preparation:

1. In a mixing bowl, season the beef with salt and pepper.
2. Prepare the slow cooker with cooking spray, and combine the onion powder, apple cider vinegar, garlic, and ketchup in the basin of the cooker. Remember to use a surface-friendly utensil.
3. Add the seasoned beef and combine gently.
4. Cover, and cook on HIGH for 4 hours.
5. Serve hot.

Nutrition facts per serving

Calories 376, Carbs 6.3 g, Fat 14.8 g, Protein 47.3 g, Sodium 238 mg

Beef Tomato Meal

Servings: 2 (refrigerate leftovers) - Prep. time: 5–8 minutes –
Cooking time: 6 hours

Ingredients:

¾ pound boneless beef short ribs, trimmed and cubed
Salt and pepper to taste
1 tablespoon olive oil
2 cups tomatoes, chopped
1 ½ tablespoons tomato paste
¼ cup white onion, peeled and sliced
½ teaspoon dried oregano

Preparation:

1. In a mixing bowl, season the beef with salt and pepper.
2. In a skillet or saucepan, heat the olive oil and evenly brown the meat chunks, 4–5 minutes.
3. Place the beef chunks in the slow cooker, and add the other ingredients. Stir the ingredients gently to combine.
4. Cook on LOW for 6 hours.
5. When the time is up, take out the meat and shred it with two forks. Add it back to the cooking liquid. Allow it to steep in the sauce until you are ready to eat.
6. Serve hot.

Nutrition facts per serving

Calories 292, Carbs 12.6 g, Fat 11 g, Protein 16 g, Sodium 56 mg

Fish & Seafood Recipes

Tangy Asparagus Tilapia

Servings: 2 - Prep. time: 10–15 minutes - Cooking time: 4 hours

Ingredients:
3 tilapia fillets
Zest from 1 lemon
Salt and pepper to taste
¼ cup lemon juice
1 ½ tablespoons butter
1 small bunch of asparagus

Preparation:
1. Make 3 aluminum foil pieces big enough to wrap one tilapia fillet each.
2. Place each fillet on a piece of aluminum foil, and sprinkle it with the zest, salt and pepper, and lemon juice.
3. Top each fillet with an equal portion of the butter, and arrange the asparagus spears on top. Gently fold the aluminum foil over each fillet, and make a closed pack by crimping the edges.
4. Place them in a slow cooker.
5. Cover, and cook on HIGH for 4 hours.
6. Being mindful of the escaping steam, open the foil packets. Flake the fish with forks, and serve.

Nutrition facts per serving
Calories 324, Carbs 19.7 g, Fat 24 g, Protein 58.7 g, Sodium 311 mg

Broccoli Salmon

Servings: 2 - Prep. time: 5–8 minutes - Cooking time: 3 hours

Ingredients:
2 tablespoons low-sodium soy sauce
2 tablespoons maple syrup
2 tablespoons lemon juice
1 pound broccoli florets
2 medium-sized salmon fillets
Salt and pepper to taste

Preparation:
1. In a mixing bowl, thoroughly combine the soy sauce, maple syrup, and lemon juice.
2. Arrange the broccoli and the salmon in the slow cooker, and season with salt and pepper.
3. Top with the sauce, and stir gently to combine.
4. Cover, and cook on LOW for 3 hours.
5. Serve hot, and enjoy!

Nutrition facts per serving
Calories 331, Carbs 11.6 g, Fat 9.2 g, Protein 23 g, Sodium 647 mg

Jalapeño Spicy Tuna

Servings: 2 - Prep. time: 5–8 minutes - Cooking time: 4 hours

Ingredients:

1 tablespoon olive oil
2-3 jalapeño peppers, membrane and seeds removed and finely diced
1 red bell peppers, trimmed and chopped
1 garlic clove, minced
¾ pound tuna loin, cubed
Salt and black pepper

Preparation:

1. Grease the inside cooking surface of the slow cooker with the olive oil.
2. In it, combine all the ingredients except the tuna.
3. Cook on LOW for 3 hours and 45 minutes.
4. Season the tuna with salt and pepper. Open the lid and add the tuna, spooning some of the sauce over the fish.
5. Cook on HIGH for 15 minutes.
6. Serve hot.

Nutrition facts per serving

Calories 202, Carbs 16.3 g, Fat 4.1 g, Protein 4.5 g, Sodium 127 mg

Spiced Soy Shrimps

Servings: 2 - Prep. time: 5–8 minutes - Cooking time: 45 minutes

Ingredients:
8 ounces shrimp, peeled, deveined, and rinsed
1 teaspoon salt
¼ teaspoon black pepper
1 teaspoon smoked paprika
¼ teaspoon red pepper flakes, crushed
3 teaspoons garlic, minced
2 tablespoons low-sodium soy sauce

Preparation:
1. In a mixing bowl, season the shrimp with the salt and black pepper.
2. In the slow cooker, combine the paprika, red pepper flakes, garlic, and soy sauce.
3. Cook on HIGH for 30 minutes.
4. Open the lid and add the seasoned shrimp.
5. Cover, and cook on HIGH for 15 more minutes.
6. Serve warm!

Nutrition facts per serving
Calories 192, Carbs 2.6 g, Fat 12 g, Protein 23.3 g, Sodium 824 mg

Coconut Clams

Servings: 2 - Prep. time: 5–8 minutes - Cooking time: 6 hours

Ingredients:
¼ cup coconut milk
2 eggs, whisked
1 tablespoon olive oil
10 ounces canned clams, chopped
1 green bell pepper, chopped
1 yellow onion, chopped
Salt and black pepper to taste

Preparation:
1. Combine all the ingredients in the slow cooker.
2. Cover, and cook on LOW for 6 hours.
3. Divide among serving bowls or plates and enjoy!

Nutrition facts per serving
Calories 271, Carbs 16 g, Fat 4.2 g, Protein 7.6 g, Sodium 607 mg

Orange Vinegar Salmon

*Servings: 2 (refrigerate leftovers) - Prep. time: 10–15 minutes –
Cooking time: 2 hours*

Ingredients:
1 tablespoon Dijon mustard
3 tablespoons orange juice
¼ cup apple cider vinegar
4 salmon fillets
Salt and pepper to taste
4 oranges, peeled and segmented

Preparation:
1. In a bowl, mix the mustard, orange juice, and apple cider vinegar.
2. Lay out 4 aluminum foil pieces big enough to wrap one fillet each.
3. Place each fillet on a piece of aluminum foil, and season with salt and pepper. Top with some sauce and orange segments.
4. Gently fold the aluminum foil over each fillet, and make a closed pack by crimping the edges.
5. Place them in a slow cooker.
6. Cook on HIGH for 2 hours.
7. Being mindful of the steam, open the foil packets. Flake the fish with forks, and serve.

Nutrition facts per serving
Calories 123, Carbs 2.8 g, Fat 6.8 g, Protein 19 g, Sodium 73 mg

Tomato Cod

Servings: 2 - Prep. time: 5–8 minutes - Cooking time: 1 to 1 ½ hours

Ingredients:

6 ounces cod fillets, cut into 2-inch pieces
Salt and pepper to taste
A sprinkle of red chili flakes (or more to taste)
1 ½ teaspoons garlic, minced
1 can diced tomatoes
1 white onion, peeled and sliced
¼ cup chicken broth

Preparation:

1. In a mixing bowl, season the cod with salt, pepper, and red chili flakes.
2. Add the remaining ingredients and mix well.
3. Spoon the mixture into the slow cooker.
4. Cook on HIGH for 1 to 1 ½ hours.
5. Serve, and enjoy!

Nutrition facts per serving
Calories 221, Carbs 6.3 g, Fat 5.8 g, Protein 34.6 g, Sodium 176 mg

Pork & Lamb Recipes

Sweet Potato Chops

Servings: 2 - Prep. time: 10–15 minutes - Cooking time: 7–8 hours

Ingredients:
2 bone-in pork chops, about 8 ounces each
Salt and pepper to taste
2 sweet potatoes, peeled and diced
Zest of 1 orange
Pinch ground nutmeg
½ cup low-sodium chicken broth

Preparation:
1. In a mixing bowl, season the pork chops with the salt and pepper.
2. Place the sweet potatoes in the slow cooker, and mix in the orange zest, nutmeg, and broth in it. Stir the ingredients gently to combine well using a wooden spatula.
3. Add the seasoned pork chops and combine gently.
4. Cover, and cook on LOW for 7–8 hours.
5. Serve hot!

Nutrition facts per serving
Calories 527, Carbs 43.6 g, Fat 7 g, Protein 36 g, Sodium 164 mg

Cider, Apple & Onion Chops

Servings: 2 - Prep. time: 10 minutes - Cooking time: 6–8 hours

Ingredients:
2 bone-in pork chops
Salt and pepper to taste
1 apple, cored, peeled, and cut into 8 wedges
1 sweet onion, make thick rings
1 teaspoon thyme
¼ cup apple cider (may substitute apple juice)
Optional: mashed potatoes, for serving

Preparation:
1. Place the pork chops in the slow cooker, and season with salt and pepper.
2. Add the apple, onion, thyme, and apple cider.
3. Cook on LOW for 6–8 hours; until the pork cooked through and fork tender.
4. Serve hot, with mashed potatoes, if desired.

Nutrition facts per serving
Calories 284, Carbs 22.4 g, Fat 5 g, Protein 21.2 g, Sodium 523 mg

Green Bean Garlic Chops

Servings: 2 - Prep. time: 5–8 minutes - Cooking time: 8 hours

Ingredients:
1 teaspoon olive oil
2 bone-in pork chops, about 8 ounces each
3 cups whole green beans, stems removed
Salt and pepper to taste
2 teaspoons ginger, minced
1 teaspoon garlic, minced
¼ cup low-sodium soy sauce
½ cup low-sodium vegetable or chicken broth

Preparation:
1. Grease the inside cooking surface of the slow cooker with the olive oil.
2. Add the pork chops and green beans, and season them with salt and pepper.
3. Add the ginger, garlic, soy sauce, and broth. Stir the ingredients gently to combine them well, using a wooden spatula.
4. Cook on LOW for 8 hours.
5. Serve hot.

Nutrition facts per serving
Calories 332, Carbs 17.1 g, Fat 4 g, Protein 34.8 g, Sodium 1926 mg

Rosemary Peach Pork

Servings: 2 - Prep. time: 10 minutes - Cooking time: 6–8 hours

Ingredients:
1 pound pork tenderloin
Salt and pepper to taste
2 peaches, peeled and cut into small wedges
½ red onion, halved and thinly sliced
1 sprig rosemary, needles only

Preparation:
1. Season the tenderloin with the salt and pepper.
2. Place it in the slow cooker, and add the peaches, onion, and rosemary.
3. Cook on LOW for 6–8 hours, until the meat cooked through.
4. Slice, and serve.

Nutrition facts per serving
Calories 373, Carbs 12 g, Fat 3.2 g, Protein 58.8 g, Sodium 243 mg

Balsamic Glazed Pork

Servings: 2 - Prep. time: 5–8 minutes - Cooking time: 6–8 hours

Ingredients:
1 pound pork tenderloin
Salt and pepper to taste
½ red onion, halved and sliced thin
4 carrots, make small pieces
2 garlic cloves, minced
¼ cup balsamic vinegar
½ cup low-sodium chicken or vegetable broth

Preparation:
1. Season the tenderloin with salt and pepper.
2. Place it in the slow cooker, and add the onion, carrots, and garlic.
3. Add the vinegar and broth. Stir gently to combine.
4. Cook on LOW for 6–8 hours, until the meat is cooked through.
5. Slice and serve warm. Enjoy!

Nutrition facts per serving
Calories 397, Carbs 15.8 g, Fat 4 g, Protein 61 g, Sodium 357 mg

Lamb Spinach Curry

*Servings: 2 (refrigerate leftovers) - Prep. time: 5–8 minutes –
Cooking time: 3 ½ hours*

Ingredients:
1 tablespoon olive oil
1 pound lamb, trimmed of fat and diced
5 teaspoons curry powder
Salt, to taste
2 cups sugar-free marinara sauce
½ cup water
6 ounces baby spinach

Preparation:
1. In a skillet or saucepan, heat the olive oil and evenly sear the lamb chunks.
2. Season with the curry powder and salt, and cook for about 7–8 minutes, stirring occasionally.
3. In the slow cooker, combine all the ingredients EXCEPT the spinach.
4. Cook on HIGH for 3 hours, and then add the spinach.
5. Cook on HIGH for 30 minutes.
6. Serve, and enjoy!

Nutrition facts per serving
Calories 310, Carbs 8.2 g, Fat 17 g, Protein 33 g, Sodium 364 mg

Lamb Garlic Tomato

Servings: 2 (refrigerate leftovers) - Prep. time: 5–8 minutes –
Cooking time: 5 hours, 20 minutes

Ingredients:
2 pounds lamb shoulder, diced
4 tomatoes, chopped
2 cloves garlic, minced
1 tablespoon ground cinnamon
Salt and pepper to taste
½ cup water
Large bunch cilantro leaves, chopped

Preparation:
1. In the slow cooker, combine the lamb, tomatoes, garlic, cinnamon, salt and pepper, and ½ cup of water. Stir the ingredients gently to combine.
2. Cook on LOW for 5 hours.
3. Add the cilantro leaves, and stir briefly.
4. Cover, and cook on LOW for 20 minutes.
5. Serve and enjoy!

Nutrition facts per serving
Calories 356, Carbs 4 g, Fat 27.2 g, Protein 39 g, Sodium 146 mg

Brown Rice and Lamb

Servings: 2 - Prep. time: 5–8 minutes - Cooking time: 8 hours

Ingredients:
12 ounces boneless lamb shoulder, cut in small cubes
2 tablespoons honey
2 tablespoons low sodium soy sauce
1 teaspoon olive oil
1 cup low sodium chicken broth
½ cup brown rice
1 scallion, white and green parts, sliced thin

Preparation:
1. In a mixing bowl, season the lamb with honey and soy sauce. Coat well.
2. Grease the inside of the slow cooker with the olive oil.
3. Add the lamb mixture, the broth, rice, and scallions. Mix well.
4. Cover, and cook on LOW for 8 hours.
5. Divide among serving bowls or plates, and enjoy!

Nutrition facts per serving
Calories 563, Carbs 53.8 g, Fat 5 g, Protein 48.6 g, Sodium 1048 mg

Vegetarian & Vegan Recipes

Tomato Eggplant Stew

Servings: 2 - Prep. time: 5–8 minutes - Cooking time: 8 hours

Ingredients:

1 small eggplant, roughly chopped
12 ounces canned tomatoes, chopped
1 small red onion, chopped
½ tablespoon smoked paprika
1 teaspoon ground cumin
1 cup veggie stock
Salt and pepper to taste

Preparation:

1. In the slow cooker, combine all the ingredients, and stir to combine.
2. Cook on LOW for 8 hours.
3. Serve hot!

Nutrition facts per serving

Calories 261, Carbs 14 g, Fat 4.2 g, Protein 7 g, Sodium 233 mg

Butternut Squash Soup

Servings: 2 (refrigerate leftovers) - Prep. time: 10 minutes
Cooking time: 4 hours

Ingredients:
5 cups butternut squash, cubed
2 cloves garlic
1 small onion, chopped
1 pinch freshly ground nutmeg
Water, about 3 cups or veggie stock
Salt and pepper to taste
¼ cup heavy cream, optional

Preparation:
4. In the slow cooker, add the squash, garlic, and onion. Just cover with water or veggie stock. Season with salt and pepper to taste. Add nutmeg and stir to combine.
5. Cook on LOW for 3-4 hours or HIGH for 1 ½ -2 hours.
6. Once the soup is cooked, squash should be very tender, use an immersion blender to blend the soup until the desired consistency.
7. For a creamier soup, if desired, add the heavy cream in the last half hour of cooking. Stir to combine.
8. Taste and adjust the seasoning with salt and pepper and nutmeg if necessary.
9. Serve hot!

Nutrition facts per serving (with vegie stock – no cream)
Calories 187, Carbs 43 g, Fat 0.2 g, Protein 10 g, Sodium 933 mg

Cheese & Cream Cauliflower Soup

Servings: 2 - Prep. time: 5–8 minutes - Cooking time: 4 hours

Ingredients:
1 teaspoon olive oil
2 cups chicken stock
1 cauliflower head, cut in small florets
1 teaspoon minced garlic
½ cup heavy cream
2 ounces cheddar cheese, grated

Preparation:
1. Grease the inside of the slow cooker with the olive oil.
2. Add all the ingredients EXCEPT the cream and cheese. Stir to combine.
3. Cook on LOW for 4 hours.
4. After the timer reads zero, open the lid and carefully transfer the cooked mixture to a blender. Process until smooth, and pour it back into the slow cooker.
5. Stir in the cream and cheese, and let sit until the cheese is melted.
6. Serve!

Nutrition facts per serving
Calories 292, Carbs 6.2 g, Fat 24.7 g, Protein 10 g, Sodium 736 mg

Sweet Green Beans

Servings: 2 - Prep. time: 5–8 minutes - Cooking time: 2 hours

Ingredients:
2 tablespoons brown sugar
1 tablespoon low-sodium soy sauce
4 cups green beans, trimmed
2 tablespoons butter
Salt and pepper to taste

Preparation:
1. Combine all the ingredients in the slow cooker.
2. Cook on LOW for 2 hours.
3. Serve this as a side to your main dish, and enjoy!

Nutrition facts per serving
Calories 237, Carbs 10 g, Fat 6.2 g, Protein 6 g, Sodium 147 mg

Spinach Bean Cassoulet

Servings: 2 - Prep. time: 5–8 minutes - Cooking time: 6–7 hours

Ingredients:
1 cup onion, minced
1 teaspoon olive oil
2 (15-ounce) cans navy beans, drained and rinsed
¼ cup celery, minced
1 teaspoon fresh sage, minced
1 tablespoon garlic, minced
1 cup low-sodium vegetable broth
¾ cup spinach, chopped

Preparation:
1. Combine all the ingredients EXCEPT the spinach in the slow cooker, and stir gently to combine.
2. Cook on LOW for 6 hours, and then open the lid and add the spinach.
3. Cover, and cook on LOW for 30 minutes.
4. Serve, and enjoy!

Nutrition facts per serving
Calories 563, Carbs 48.3 g, Fat 1 g, Protein 54.6 g, Sodium 876 mg

Almond Bean Dip

Servings: 2 (refrigerate leftovers) - Prep. time: 5–8 minutes –
Cooking time: 8 hours

Ingredients:
1 cup slivered almonds
½ cup great northern beans, dried
2 cup water
¼ teaspoon pepper
½ teaspoon salt
1 ½ teaspoons nutritional yeast

Preparation:
1. In the slow cooker, combine the almonds, beans, and water.
2. Cook on LOW for 8 hours.
3. When finished, transfer the cooked mixture to a blender.
4. Add the pepper, salt, and yeast. Blend until smooth.
5. Enjoy this nutritious dip with your favorite crackers, snacks, or veggie sticks.

Nutrition facts per serving
Calories 276, Carbs 22.4 g, Fat 18 g, Protein 13 g, Sodium 462 mg

Cheesy Tofu & Peas

Servings: 2 - Prep. time: 15–20 minutes - Cooking time: 8 hours

Ingredients:
8 ounces marinated tofu
1 cup frozen peas, thawed
½ cup onion, minced
Salt and pepper to taste
1 ½ cups mashed potatoes
2 tablespoons sharp cheddar cheese, shredded

Preparation:
1. In the slow cooker, combine the tofu, peas, onion, and salt and pepper.
2. Add the mashed potatoes and stir them in.
3. Close the lid and make sure that the valve is sealed properly.
4. Cover, and cook on LOW for 7 ½ hours.
5. Sprinkle the cheese on top, and cover. Cook 30 minutes more on LOW, until the cheese is melted.

Nutrition facts per serving
Calories 464, Carbs 53 g, Fat 6.3 g, Protein 31.7 g, Sodium 337 mg

Cauliflower Lentils

Servings: 2 - Prep. time: 10 minutes - Cooking time: 8 hours

Ingredients:
1 cup cauliflower florets
1 cup lentils
Zest of 1 lemon
1 tablespoon roasted garlic, chopped
1 tablespoon rosemary
1 tablespoon olive oil
Sea salt and pepper to taste
3 cups low-sodium vegetable broth
Juice of 1 lemon

Preparation:
1. In the slow cooker, combine all the ingredients EXCEPT the lemon juice.
2. Cook on LOW for 8 hours.
3. When the time is up, stir in the lemon juice, and serve.

Nutrition facts per serving
Calories 483, Carbs 64.6 g, Fat 2 g, Protein 34 g, Sodium 187 mg

Kale and Chickpeas

Servings: 2 - Prep. time: 5 minutes - Cooking time: 4 hours

Ingredients:
½ cup canned chickpeas, drained and rinsed
2 cups kale, trimmed and washed
2-3 teaspoons Italian herb blend
½ cup plum tomatoes, roughly chopped
1 ½ cups low-sodium vegetable broth
⅛ teaspoon sea salt
½ cup quinoa
Optional: crusty, whole-grain bread, for serving

Preparation:
1. Combine all the ingredients in the slow cooker.
2. Cook on LOW for 4 hours.
3. Divide into serving bowls, and enjoy with a slice of crusty bread.

Nutrition facts per serving
Calories 341, Carbs 52 g, Fat 1 g, Protein 18.8 g, Sodium 452 mg

Delicious Desserts

Creamy Chocolate Treat

Servings: 2 - Prep. time: 5–8 minutes - Cooking time: 1 hour

Ingredients:
2 ounces dark chocolate, cut in small chunks
¼ cup low-fat cream
½ teaspoon sugar

Preparation:
1. In your slow cooker, combine all the ingredients.
2. Cook on HIGH for 1 hour.
3. Spoon the mixture into a serving bowl, and chill in the refrigerator.
4. Serve cold.

Nutrition facts per serving
Calories 115, Carbs 5.6 g, Fat 10 g, Protein 2.4 g, Sodium 136 mg

Cocoa Cherry Dessert

Servings: 2 - Prep. time: 5–8 minutes - Cooking time: 2 hours

Ingredients:
2-3 tablespoons maple syrup
½ pound cherries, pitted and halved
¼ cup cocoa powder
½ cup red cherry juice
1 cup water

Preparation:
1. Combine all the ingredients in the slow cooker. Mix well.
2. Cook on HIGH for 2 hours.
3. When the time is up, transfer the cooked mixture into a bowl, and refrigerate.
4. Serve chilled!

Nutrition facts per serving
Calories 243, Carbs 44.6 g, Fat 2.3 g, Protein 3 g, Sodium 38 mg

Cinnamon Peach Cobbler

Servings: 2 - Prep. time: 5–8 minutes - Cooking time: 4 hours

Ingredients:
2 cups peaches, peeled, seeded, and sliced
½ teaspoon ground cinnamon
2 tablespoons sugar, divided
¼ cup milk
1 teaspoon vanilla extract
Cooking spray

Preparation:
1. In a mixing bowl, combine the peach slices, cinnamon, and 1 tablespoon of sugar. Mix well.
2. In another bowl, combine the milk with the remaining sugar and the vanilla extract.
3. Grease the inside of the slow cooker with the cooking spray.
4. Add the peach mixture, and top with the milk. Gently combine.
5. Cover, and cook on LOW for 4 hours.
6. Divide the cobbler into bowls, and serve warm.

Nutrition facts per serving
Calories 187, Carbs 32.6 g, Fat 3.4 g, Protein 4 g, Sodium 28 mg

Cinnamon Apple Delight

Servings: 2 - Prep. time: 5–8 minutes - Cooking time: 4 hours

Ingredients:
¼ teaspoon cinnamon, ground
2 tablespoons sugar
2 apples, cored, peeled and make cubes
2 tablespoons olive oil
½ tablespoon lemon juice
½ teaspoon vanilla extract
Optional: whipped cream or vanilla yogurt, for serving

Preparation:
1. In a mixing bowl, thoroughly combine the cinnamon and sugar.
2. In the slow cooker, combine the apple, olive oil, lemon juice, and vanilla.
3. Sprinkle the cinnamon sugar over the apple mixture.
4. Cook on HIGH for 4 hours.
5. Divide among serving bowls or plates, add topping if desired, and enjoy!

Nutrition facts per serving
Calories 198, Carbs 14.5 g, Fat 4 g, Protein 3.3 g, Sodium 9 mg

Tangy Ginger Pears

Servings: 2 - Prep. time: 5–8 minutes - Cooking time: 4 hours

Ingredients:
2 pears, peeled and cored
1 cup orange juice
2 tablespoons maple syrup
1 teaspoon ground cinnamon
½ tablespoon grated ginger

Preparation:
1. Combine all the ingredients in the slow cooker.
2. Cover, and cook on LOW for 4 hours.
3. Divide among serving bowls and enjoy!

Nutrition facts per serving
Calories 252, Carbs 12.6 g, Fat 1.7 g, Protein 4 g, Sodium 23 mg

Recipe Index

Also by Louise Davidson

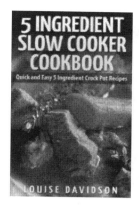

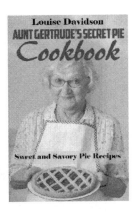

Appendix
Cooking Conversion Charts

1. Measuring Equivalent Chart

Type	Imperial	Imperial	Metric
Weight	1 dry ounce		28g
	1 pound	16 dry ounces	0.45 kg
Volume	1 teaspoon		5 ml
	1 dessert spoon	2 teaspoons	10 ml
	1 tablespoon	3 teaspoons	15 ml
	1 Australian tablespoon	4 teaspoons	20 ml
	1 fluid ounce	2 tablespoons	30 ml
	1 cup	16 tablespoons	240 ml
	1 cup	8 fluid ounces	240 ml
	1 pint	2 cups	470 ml
	1 quart	2 pints	0.95 l
	1 gallon	4 quarts	3.8 l
Length	1 inch		2.54 cm

* Numbers are rounded to the closest equivalent

2. Oven Temperature Equivalent Chart

Fahrenheit (°F)	Celsius (°C)	Gas Mark
220	100	
225	110	1/4
250	120	1/2
275	140	1
300	150	2
325	160	3
350	180	4
375	190	5
400	200	6
425	220	7
450	230	8
475	250	9
500	260	

* Celsius (°C) = T (°F)-32] * 5/9

** Fahrenheit (°F) = T (°C) * 9/5 + 32

*** Numbers are rounded to the closest equivalent

Made in United States
Orlando, FL
19 December 2022

27343029R00039